BOOK 4

THE NEW NATION
1789–1850

BOOK 5

LIBERTY FOR ALL?
1820–1860

STUDENT STUDY GUIDE
TO THE REVISED THIRD EDITION

GRADE FIVE

OXFORD
UNIVERSITY PRESS

OXFORD
UNIVERSITY PRESS

Oxford University Press, Inc., publishes works that further
Oxford University's objective of excellence
in research, scholarship, and education.

Oxford New York
Auckland Cape Town Dar es Salaam Hong Kong Karachi
Kuala Lumpur Madrid Melbourne Mexico City Nairobi
New Delhi Shanghai Taipei Toronto

With offices in
Argentina Austria Brazil Chile Czech Republic France Greece
Guatemala Hungary Italy Japan Poland Portugal Singapore
South Korea Switzerland Thailand Turkey Ukraine Vietnam

Copyright © 2005 by Oxford University Press

Published by Oxford University Press, Inc.
198 Madison Avenue, New York, New York, 10016

www.oup.com

Oxford is a registered trademark of Oxford University Press

Writers: Ruth Ashby, Scott Ingram
Project Director: Jacqueline A. Ball
Education Consultant: Diane L. Brooks, Ed.D.
Casper Grathwohl, Publisher

Library of Congress Cataloging-in-Publication Data is available
ISBN 13: 978-0-19-976733-5

Printed in the United States of America
on acid-free paper

Dear Parents, Guardians, and Students:

This study guide has been created to increase student enjoyment and understanding of *A History of US*.

The study guide offers a wide variety of interactive exercises to support every chapter. At the back of the guide are several copies of a library/media center research log students can use to organize research projects and assignments. Parents or other family members can participate in activities marked "With a Parent or Partner." Adults can help in other ways, too. One important way is to encourage students to create and use a history journal as they work through the exercises in the guide. The journal can simply be an off-the-shelf notebook or three-ring binder used only for this purpose. Some students might like to customize their journals with markers, colored paper, drawings, or computer graphics. No matter what it looks like, a journal is a student's very own place to organize thoughts, practice writing, and make notes on important information. It will serve as a personal report of ongoing progress that a teacher can evaluate regularly. When completed, it will be a source of satisfaction and accomplishment.

Sincerely,

Casper Grathwohl
Publisher

This book belongs to:

_____

CONTENTS

How to Use the Student Study Guide   **6**

Graphic Organizers   **8**

Reports and Special Projects   **10**

Book Four

Preface—Getting a Nation Started   **11**

The democratic ideals set forth in the Declaration of Independence and the Constitution will be both challenged and fulfilled as the new nation begins.

Chapters 1 and 2—The Father of Our Country/About Being President   **13**

After his unanimous election as the nation's first president, George Washington set off on a triumphant journey to his inauguration ceremony. In his new job, Washington set many important precedents. One of his first tasks was to organize a group of advisors, or cabinet.

Chapter 3—The Parties Begin   **15**

Thomas Jefferson and Alexander Hamilton, who disagreed about how the United States should be governed, founded the nation's first two political parties.

Chapter 5—Counting Noses   **17**

The Census of 1790 counted all the citizens in the rapidly growing nation.

Chapter 10—Meet Mr. Jefferson   **19**

President Thomas Jefferson wanted to be a truly democratic president, a "man of the people."

Chapter 11—Meriwether and William—Or Lewis and Clark   **21**

The Lewis and Clark Expedition explores the lands of the Louisiana Purchase.

Chapters 12, 13, 14—An Orator in a Red Jacket Speaks/The Great Tekamthi, Also Called Tecumseh/Oseola   **23**

Iroquois chief Sagoyewatha spoke eloquently on behalf of his people. Shawnee chief Tecumseh tried to unite all Indian tribes against the white settlers who were invading their land. When he was a boy, Osceola witnessed a fierce civil war pitting Creeks who wanted to adopt a white way of life against those who did not.

Chapter 15—The Revolutionary War Part II, or the War of 1812   **25**

The War of 1812 convinced the world that the United States could hold its own against the greatest army and navy on earth.

Chapter 21—Yankee Ingenuity: Cotton and Muskets   **27**

The Industrial Revolution transformed the lives of Americans in both North and South.

Chapter 22—Going Places   **29**

New roads and canals quickly and cheaply transported goods and people from place to place.

Chapter 23—Teakettle Power   **31**

American and British inventors figured out ways to harness steampower to drive steamboats and trains.

Chapters 24 and 25—Making Words/A Time to Weep   **33**

Sequoyah invented a written Cherokee alphabet and gave his people a new way to communicate. Even though the Supreme Court ruled Indian removal unconstitutional, President Andrew Jackson sent the Cherokees west on the Trail of Tears.

Chapters 30 and 31—The King and His People/Abolitionists Want to End Slavery   **35**

"King Cotton" ruled the South after the invention of the cotton gin and guaranteed the continuation of slavery. Northern abolitionists alarmed southern slave owners by demanding an end to slavery.

Chapter 32—Frederick Douglass   **37**

Frederick Douglass escaped from slavery and became an important abolitionist.

Book Five

Chapter 1—The Long Way West   39

In the early 19th century, most Americans regarded the Great Plains as a desert and knew little of the land beyond. They thought the land of the Louisiana Purchase was uninhabitable and were happy to leave it to the Native Americans

Chapter 2—Mountain Men   41

A group of rough-and-tumble fur traders known as mountain men took the lead in blazing trails across Native American lands west of the Mississippi River.

Chapters 3 and 4—Riding the Trail to Santa Fe/Susan Magoffin's Diary   43

U.S explorers also found their way into lands claimed by Mexico. The lure of profit led them to carve out a trail to Santa Fe, paving the way for the later U.S> takeover of New Mexico. Susan Magoffin was among the "foreign invaders" who traveled into Spanish-speaking New Mexico. Her brother James helped in the bloodless U.S. takeover of the Mexican territory.

Chapters 5 and 6—Pioneers: Taking the Trail West/Getting There   45

Dreams of fertile lands fueled the pioneers who traveled the Oregon Trail—a trail marked by graves, animal carcasses, and discarded personal treasures. The dangers of travel along the Oregon Trail forged close bonds among pioneers. Following a tradition started by Pilgrims, many groups wrote compacts to ensure that they carried into the wilderness governments based on law.

Chapter 7—Latter-Day Saints   47

The Mormons were pioneers in search of religious freedom. Their settlement of the Utah territory increased the culture pluralism of our country.

Chapter 8—Coast-to Coast Destiny   49

The idea of manifest destiny was fueled by the writing of California traveler Richard Henry Dana. President James Polk began diplomatic probes to wrest this land from the Mexicans.

Chapter 9—A Hero of His Times   51

John Frémont played a key role in securing California for America. He first created interest in the territory and then, in a controversial manner, helped America claim it.

Chapter 10—Texas: Tempting and Beautiful   53

First, the Spanish took what is now Texas from the Indians. Then anglos and tejanos (Mexican Texans) took it from Mexico. For nearly a decade, Texas existed as an independent republic.

Chapter 11—Fighting Over a Border   55

Hotheads on both sides of the Rio Grande itched to do battle. In the United States, the desire for land proved stronger than the desire for peace. The result was war.

Chapter 12—There's Gold in Them Hills   57

The ink had barely dried on the Treaty of Guadalupe Hidalgo when a single word blazed across the headlines: Gold! The word proved a magnet as people scrambled to California.

Scorecard
Library Media Rubrics

HOW TO USE THE STUDENT STUDY GUIDES TO
A HISTORY OF US

One word describes A History of US: stories. Every book in this series is packed with stories about people who built a brand new country like none before. You will meet presidents and politicians, artists and inventors, ordinary people who did amazing things and had wonderful adventures. The best part is that all the stories are true. All the people are real.

As you read this book, you can enjoy the stories while you build valuable thinking and writing skills. The book will help you meet history-social science content standards and pass important tests. The sample pages below show special features in all the History of US books. Take a look!

Before you read

- Have a notebook or extra paper and a pen handy to make a history journal. A dictionary and thesaurus will help you too.

- Read the chapter title and predict what you will learn from the chapter. Note that often the author often adds humor to her titles with plays on words or **puns**, as in this title.

- Study all maps, photos, and their captions closely. The captions often contain important information you won't find in the text.

27 Howe Billy Wished France Wouldn't Join In

A **hoop-stay** was part of the stiffening in a skirt; a **japon** was part of a corset. **Matrons** are married women. The **misses** are single girls; **swains** and **beaux** are young men or boyfriends. **Making love** meant flirting. **British Grenadiers** are part of the royal household's infantry.

General Howe had already served in America. In 1759 he led Wolfe's troops to seize Quebec.

Sir William Howe (who was sometimes called Billy Howe) was in charge of all the British forces in America. It was Howe who drove the American army from Long Island to Manhattan. Then he chased it across another river to New Jersey. And, after that, he forced George Washington to flee on— to Pennsylvania. It looked as if it was all over for the rebels. In New Jersey, some 3,000 Americans took an oath of allegiance to the king. But Washington got lucky again. The Europeans didn't like to fight in cold weather.

Sir William settled in New York City for the winter season. Howe thought Washington and his army were done for and could be

Swarming with Beaux

Rebecca Franks was the daughter of a wealthy Philadelphia merchant. Her father was the king's agent in Pennsylvania, and the family were Loyalists. Rebecca visited New York when it was occupied by the British. Her main interest in the war was that it meant New York was full of handsome officers:

My Dear Abby, By the by, few New York ladies know how to entertain company in their own houses unless they introduce the card tables....I don't know a woman or girl that can chat above half an hour, and that on the form of a cap, the colour of a ribbon or the set of a hoop-stay or jupon....Here, you enter a room with a formal set curtsey and after the how do's, 'tis a fine, or a bad day, and those trifling nothings are finish'd, all's a dead calm till the cards are introduced, when you see pleasure dancing in the eyes of all the matrons....The misses, if they have a favorite swain, frequently decline playing for the pleasure of making love....Yesterday the Grenadiers had a race at the Flatlands, and in the afternoon this house swarm'd with beaux and some very smart ones. How the girls wou'd have envy'd me cou'd they have peep'd and seen how I was surrounded.

126

6

As you read

- Keep a list of questions.

- Note the bold-faced definitions in the margins. They tell you the meanings of important words and terms – ones you may not know.

- Look up other unfamiliar words in a dictionary.

- Note other sidebars or special features. They contain additional information for your enjoyment and to build your understanding. Often sidebars and features contain quotations from primary source documents such as a diary or letter, like this one. Sometimes the primary source item is a cartoon or picture.

finished off in springtime. Besides, Billy Howe loved partying. And some people say he liked the Americans and didn't approve of George III's politics. For reasons that no one is quite sure of, General Howe just took it easy.

But George Washington was no quitter. On Christmas Eve of 1776, in bitter cold, Washington got the Massachusetts fishermen to ferry his men across the Delaware River from Pennsylvania back to New Jersey. The river was clogged with huge chunks of ice. You had to be crazy, or coolly courageous, to go out into that dangerous water. The Hessians, on the other side—at Trenton, New Jersey— were so sure Washington wouldn't cross in such bad weather that they didn't patrol the river. Washington took them by complete surprise.

A week later, Washington left a few men to tend his campfires and fool the enemy. He quietly marched his army to Prince-ton, New Jersey, where he surprised and beat a British force. People in New Jersey forgot the oaths they had sworn to the king. They were Patriots again.

Those weren't big victories that Washington had won, but they certainly helped American morale. And American morale needed help. It still didn't seem as if the colonies had a chance. After all, Great Britain had the most feared army in the world. It was amazing that a group of small colonies would even attempt to fight the powerful British empire. When a large English army (9,500 men and 138 cannons) headed south from Canada in June 1777, many observers thought the rebellion would soon be over.

The army was led by one of Britain's

The Road to Saratoga

↓ ROUTES TAKEN BY BRITISH
↘ ROUTES PLANNED BY BURGOYNE
☆ BATTLE

General Burgoyne's redcoats carried far too much equipment. Each man's boots alone weighed 12 pounds. They took two months to cover 40 miles from Fort Ticonderoga to Saratoga, and lost hundreds of men to American snipers.

127

After you read

- Compare what you have learned with what you thought you would learn before you began the chapter.

The next two pages have models of graphic organizers. You will need these to do the activities for each chapter on the pages after that. Go back to the book as often as you need to. When you've finished each chapter, check off the standards in the box.

GRAPHIC ORGANIZERS

As you read and study history, geography, and the social sciences, you'll start to collect a lot of information. Using a graphic organizer is one way to make information clearer and easier to understand. You can choose from different types of organizers, depending on the information.

OUTLINE

MAIN IDEA: _____

_____

DETAIL: _____

DETAIL: _____

DETAIL: _____

MAIN IDEA: _____

_____

DETAIL: _____

DETAIL: _____

DETAIL: _____

Outline

To build an outline, first identify your main idea. Write this at the top. Then, in the lines below, list the details that support the main idea. Keep adding main ideas and details as you need to.

MAIN IDEA MAP

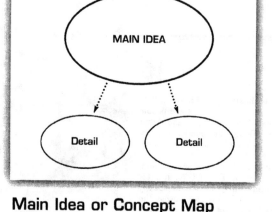

Main Idea or Concept Map

Write down your main idea or concept in the central circle. Write details in the connecting circles. You can use this form to make a word web, too.

K-W-L CHART

K	W	L
What I Know	What I Want to Know	What I Learned

K-W-L Chart

Before you read a chapter, write down what you already know about a subject in the left column. Skim the chapter. Then write what you want to know in the center column. Then write what you learned in the last column. You can make a two-column version of this. Write what you know in the left column and what you learned after reading the chapter in the right.

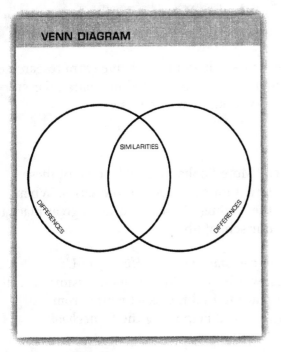

Venn Diagram

These overlapping circles show differences and similarities among topics. Each topic is shown as a circle. Any details the topics have in common go in the areas where those circles overlap. List the differences where the circles do not overlap.

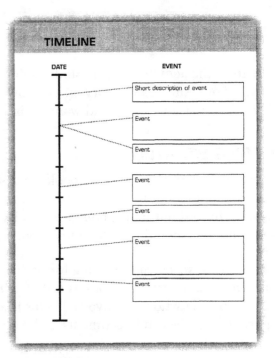

Timeline

A timeline divides a time period into equal chunks of time. Then it shows when events happened during that time. Decide how to divide up the timeline. Then write events in the boxes to the right when they happened. Connect them to the date line.

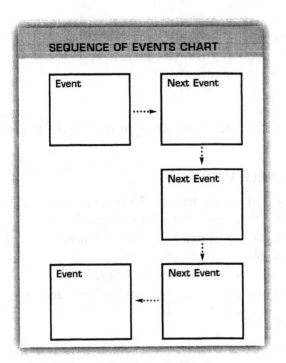

Sequence of Events Chart

Historical events bring about changes. These result in other events and changes. A sequence of events chart uses linked boxes to show how one event leads to another, and then another.

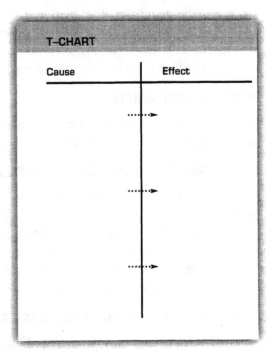

T–Chart

Use this chart to separate information into two columns. To separate causes and effects, list events, or causes, in one column. In the other column, list the change, or effect, each event brought about.

REPORTS AND SPECIAL PROJECTS

Aside from the activities in this Study Guide, your teacher may ask you to do some extra research or reading about American history on your own. Or, you might become interested in a particular story you read in *A History of US* and want to find out more. Do you know where to start?

GETTING STARTED

The back of every History of US book has a section called "More Books to Read." Some of these books are fiction and some are nonfiction. This list is different for each book in the series. When you want to find out more about a particular topic from the reading, these books are a great place to start—and you should be able to find many of them in your school library.

Also, if you're specifically looking for *primary sources*, you can start with the *History of US Sourcebook and Index*. This book is full of *primary sources*, words and evidence about history directly from the people who were involved. This is an excellent place to find the exact words from important speeches and documents. Ask your teacher if you need help using the *Sourcebook*.

DOING RESEARCH

For some of the group projects and assignments in this course, you will need to conduct research either in a library or online. When your teacher asks you to research a topic, remember the following tips:

TO FIND GOOD EVIDENCE, START WITH GOOD SOURCES

Usually, your teacher will expect you to support your research with *primary sources*. Remember that a primary source for an event comes from someone who was there when the event took place. The best evidence for projects and writing assignments always comes from *primary sources*, so if you can't seem to find any right away, keep looking.

ASK THE LIBRARIAN

Librarians are amazing people who can help you find just about anything in the library. If you get stuck, remember to ask a librarian for help.

WHEN RESEARCHING ONLINE, STICK TO CREDIBLE WEBSITES

It can be hard to decide which websites are credible and which are not. To be safe, stick with websites that both you and your teacher trust. There are plenty of online sources that have information you can trust to be correct, and usually they're names you already know. For example, you can trust the facts you get from places like pbs.org, census.gov, historychannel.com, and historyofus.com. In addition to free websites like these, check with your librarian to see which *databases and subscription-based websites* your school can access.

USE THE LIBRARY/MEDIA CENTER RESEARCH LOG

At the back of this study guide, you'll find several copies of a Library/Media Center Research Log. Take one with you to the library or media center, and keep track of your sources. Also, take time to decide how helpful and relevant those sources are.

OTHER RESOURCES

Your school and public library have lots of additional resources to help you with your research. These include videos, DVDs, software, and CDs.

Preface GETTING A NATION STARTED

SUMMARY *The democratic ideals set forth in the Declaration of Independence and the Constitution will be both challenged and fulfilled as the new nation begins.*

ACCESS

What was the United States like in its first years as a nation? In your history journal, copy the "K-W-L" chart from page 8. In the first column, write everything you already know about the nation in about the year 1790. In the middle column, write down any questions you have. As you read the next few chapters, write everything that you learn in the third column.

WORD BANK   preface   mint   Industrial Revolution

Write the correct word or phrase next to its definition.

1. The shift from hand tools to machines powered by steam and electricity:_____

2. An introduction by a writer or speaker:_____

3. To make coins out of metal: _____

WITH A PARENT OR PARTNER The prefix "pre" means "before" or "earlier than." With a parent or partner, think of as many words as you can that begin with "pre." Hint: one of them is on this page.

CRITICAL THINKING

MAIN IDEA AND SUPPORTING DETAILS   Each sentence in italics below states a main idea from the chapter. Put a check mark in the blanks in front of all of the sentences that support or tell more about the main idea.

1. *There is much to do in this newly formed nation.*

_____a. Land west of the Mississippi needs to be explored.

_____b. Farmers rise at dawn and go to bed by 8:00.

_____c. Newly arrived immigrants need homes and jobs.

2. *Some Americans are taking advantage of other Americans.*

_____a. People own slaves for economic reasons.

_____b. Indentured servants are forced to work for a master until their debts are paid off.

_____c. The Industrial Revolution will bring far-reaching changes in daily life.

3. *As the 19th century approaches, ideas are changing.*

_____a. The Southern economy is dependent on slavery.

_____b. Northern states are outlawing slavery.

_____c. Some people are beginning to think that "We the people" means people of all races, colors, and religions.

USING PRIMARY SOURCES

ANALYSIS   Read the Thomas Jefferson quote opposite page 9, then answer the following questions.

Jefferson is using a metaphor to describe different social classes. A metaphor is a comparison between two things that are not alike.

1. To what is Jefferson comparing the "mass of mankind"? _____

2. Who are the "favored few"? _____ To what are they being compared?
_____

3. In your own words, explain the meaning of this metaphor._____
_____

4. Now read the quote from Henry David Thoreau at the top of the page. He is using a metaphor, too. What is the "iron horse"? _____

5. Circle the words that tell what kinds of sounds the "iron horse" makes.

6. Circle the words that tell us what it looks like.

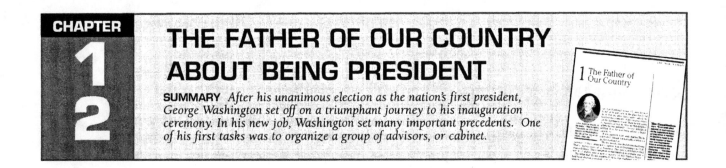

CHAPTER 1 2

THE FATHER OF OUR COUNTRY
ABOUT BEING PRESIDENT

SUMMARY *After his unanimous election as the nation's first president, George Washington set off on a triumphant journey to his inauguration ceremony. In his new job, Washington set many important precedents. One of his first tasks was to organize a group of advisors, or cabinet.*

ACCESS

George Washington is known as the "father of our country" for many different reasons. In your history journal, copy the main idea map graphic organizer from page 8. In the largest circle put George Washington's name. In the smaller circles write down the roles he played both during the revolution and during first years of the nation.

WORD BANK   precedents   inauguration   cabinet   faction   monetary

Choose words from the Word Bank to complete the sentences. One word is not used at all.

1. The president's closest advisors are called his _____.

2. Cheering crowds lined the roads as Washington traveled to New York City for his _____ as president.

3. _____ means anything having to do with money.

4. As the nation's first president, Washington set many _____ that other presidents have followed to this day.

Find the word you did not use on page 22. Then look the word up in the dictionary. Write down the definition that fits the sentence. _____

CRITICAL THINKING

WHO AM I?

Washington's cabinet was made up of extraordinary men. Use the name bank to identify the people described below. Some names are used more than once. One name is not used.

Henry Knox   Thomas Jefferson   James Madison

Alexander Hamilton   Edmund Randolph   John Adams

1. I was the first secretary of the treasury._____

2. I knew a lot about foreign affairs. _____

3. I was in charge of artillery during the Revolutionary War._____

4. I was the first vice president. _____

5. I was the first attorney general. _____

6. I was the first secretary of war._____

7. I was the first secretary of state. _____

8. I organized the country's first monetary system. _____

USING PRIMARY SOURCES

MAKING INFERENCES

Abigail Adams, wife of vice president John Adams, described Martha Washington in a letter to her sister:

> She is plain in her dress but that plainness is the best of every article. Her manners are modest and unassuming, dignified and feminine.

1. On page 20, you read that George Washington dressed very carefully for his role as president. How can you tell that Martha is dressing carefully too?

2. Write a synonym for the word "plain." _____

3. Why are "plain" clothes suitable for the wife of the president?

4. Does Abigail approve of Martha Washington? How can you tell?

5. Compare this passage to Abigail's description of George Washington on page 14. What two terms does Abigail use to describe both husband and wife?

THE PARTIES BEGIN

SUMMARY *Thomas Jefferson and Alexander Hamilton, who disagreed about how the United States should be governed, founded the nation's first two political parties.*

ACCESS

What are the two major political parties in the United States today? Which is more liberal? Which is more conservative? With a parent or partner, look up the political parties of the current president of the United States, the two senators from your state, and the representative from your congressional district. Write the names of all the politicians and the political parties they belong to in your history journal.

WORD BANK   capital   credit   capitalism   interest   default   liberal   conservative

Write the correct word next to its definition.

1. Failure to pay back a debt: _____

2. Money or other goods that are worth money: _____

3. An economic system based on private ownership and investment in business: _____

4. A viewpoint that favors traditional values and is reluctant to make changes: _____

5. A charge for borrowing money: _____

6. A viewpoint that favors civil liberties and progress and change in government: _____

7. Financial trustworthiness: _____

CRITICAL THINKING

COMPARE AND CONTRAST

The sentences below describe Thomas and Jefferson and Alexander Hamilton. Copy the model of the Venn diagram from page 9. Label once circle "Jefferson.' Label the other circle "Hamilton." Now copy the phrases below in the correct circles. The phrases that apply to only one character go in that person's circle. The phrases that describe the actions of both people go in the area where the two circles connect.

1. Liberal	5. Trusted ordinary people	9. Conservative
2. Was a Founding Father	6. Believed in strong government	10. Was a Federalist
3. Feared the masses	7. Feared strong government	11. Believed in free education
4. Was a Democratic-Republican	8. Was in Washington's cabinet	12. Wanted a government run by a wealthy elite

USING PRIMARY SOURCES

Thomas Jefferson wrote these words to describe Alexander Hamilton:

> Hamilton was, indeed, a singular character. Of acute understanding . . . honest, and honorable in all private transactions . . . yet so bewitched . . . by the British example, as to be under a thorough conviction that corruption was essential to government.

1. Based on what you know about Hamilton, what do you think Jefferson means by "acute understanding"? Circle your answer.

   a. sympathetic

   b. very intelligent

   c. stupid

   d. polite

2. Jefferson seems to think that Hamilton is

   a. a liar

   b. proud

   c. contradictory

   d. foolish

3. Why do you think Jefferson believes that the British government is corrupt?

IN YOUR OWN WORDS

In your history journal, rewrite this passage in your own words.

COUNTING NOSES

SUMMARY *The Census of 1790 counted all the citizens in the rapidly growing nation*

ASSESS

The U.S. government conducts a census every 10 years. On the Internet or in the library, look up the 2000 Census and answer the following questions in your history journal: How many people were living in the United States in 2000? How many people were living in your state? In your city or town? How many more people live in the United States today than in 1790?

WORD BANK   census   inhabitants   frontier

Choose words from the Word Bank to complete the sentences. One word is not used at all

1. An official count of the number of people who live in an area is called a _____.

2. The American _____ kept moving west as settlers moved into the Northwest and Southwest Territories.

WORD PLAY

Look up the word you did not use in the dictionary. Then write it in a sentence.

_____

What verb has the same root as this noun?_____

CRITICAL THINKING

ALL OVER THE MAP

Look at the U.S. Census of 1790 map on page 34 and answer the following questions:

1. Which state had the most inhabitants?_____ About how many did it have?

2. Which state had the fewest inhabitants? _____ About how many did it have?

_____

3. Which three states (or future states) had approximately the same number of people?

_____

4. How many more people lived in Virginia than in North Carolina? _____

5. Which three future states, in addition to the original thirteen states, were counted in the census?

_____

6. What do New York, Charleston, and Philadelphia have in common?

_____

USING PRIMARY SOURCES

In 1831, Frenchman Alexis de Tocqueville toured the United States and described a log cabin on the frontier:

> A single window with a muslin curtain; on a hearth of trodden clay an immense fire . . . a good rifle, a deerskin, and plumes of eagles' feathers; on the right hand of the chimney, a map of the United States . . . near the map, on a shelf formed by roughly hewn plank . . . a Bible . . . and two of Shakespeare's plays . . . in the center of the room, a rude table [with] . . . a teapot of British china, silver spoons, cracked teacups, and some newspapers.

MAKING INFERENCES

1. What does their choice of reading matter tell us about the family that lives in the cabin?
2. How do we know that the family is patriotic?
3. Why do you think the family brought a teapot and silver spoons into the wilderness?

MEET MR. JEFFERSON

SUMMARY *President Thomas Jefferson wanted to be a truly democratic president, a "man of the people."*

ACCESS

Thomas Jefferson was a man of many interests and talents. In your history journal, copy the main idea map graphic organizer from page 8. In the largest circle put Jefferson's name. In the smaller circles write facts that you learn about him as you read the chapter.

BUILDING BACKGROUND

Why was Jefferson already famous before he was elected president?

_____

_____

WORD BANK   predecessors   tariff   radical   protective tariff

Choose words from the Word Bank to complete the sentences.

1. Alexander Hamilton wanted a high _____ to protect American

   industry from foreign competition.

2. Washington and Adams were Jefferson's _____ in the office of the

   president of the United States.

3. A _____ is someone with extreme political views.

4. Any kind of _____ taxes imports and exports.

CRITICAL THINKING

FACT OR OPINION

A fact is a statement that can be proven. An opinion judges things or people, but it cannot be proved or disproved. Make a two-column chart in your journal. Label one column "Fact" and the other column "Opinion." Write each sentence below from the chapter in the column where it belongs.

1. "Jefferson had spent the past years fighting the Federalists and Federalist ideas."

2. "Perhaps it was that Jefferson looked for the good in people."

3. "Many people say that Alexander Hamilton was the best secretary of state ever."

4. "Jefferson spent $15 million on the Louisiana Purchase."

5. "The Louisiana Purchase happened in 1803."

6. "Hamilton was the kind of man who wanted to vote for the best-qualified person."

7. "It was Burr who challenged Hamilton to a duel."

8. "Hamilton was a man of rare talent and integrity who loved his country."

USING PRIMARY SOURCES

Eyewitnesses Nathaniel Pendleton and William P. Van Ness described the fatal duel between Alexander Hamilton and Aaron Burr on July 11, 1804:

> Asked if they were prepared [the second] gave the word present . . . and both of the parties took aim and fired in succession . . . the pistols were discharged within a few seconds of each other and the fire of Colonel Burr took effect; General Hamilton almost instantly fell, Colonel Burr then advanced toward General Hamilton with a manner and gesture that appeared to General Hamilton's friend to be expressive of regret, but without speaking turned about and withdrew.

WRITE ABOUT IT

Imagine that you are a journalist for a New York City paper and you write an article about the Hamilton–Burr duel. In your history journal, write an eye-catching headline. Then tell your reader what happened on July 11, 1804. Interview Pendleton, Van Ness, and Burr after Hamilton's death. How do you think Burr feels about what happened?

CHAPTER 11

MERIWETHER AND WILLIAM — OR LEWIS AND CLARK

SUMMARY *The Lewis and Clark Expedition explores the lands of the Louisiana Purchase.*

ACCESS

You may have heard the names "Lewis and Clark" before. But what do you really know about their famous expedition? In your history journal, copy the "K-W-L" chart from page 8. In the first column, write everything you already know about the expedition. In the middle column, write down any questions you have. As you read the chapter, write everything that you learn in the third column.

WORD BANK   mouth   source   trek   court martial

Choose words from the Word Bank to complete the sentences. One word is not used at all.

1. A military trial is called a _____.

2. The _____ of the Missouri River opens into the Mississippi River. Its

   _____ is the small streams of the Rocky Mountains.

WORD PLAY

Look up in a dictionary the word you did not use. Use that word in a sentence with one other word from the word bank.

CRITICAL THINKING

SEQUENCE OF EVENTS The sentences below list events of the Lewis and Clark Expedition. Use the text of the chapter and the map on pages 60–61 to put the events in the correct order (use "1" for the first event, and so on).

_____ Jefferson writes a set of instructions for the expedition.

_____ Sacajawea is reunited with her brother in the Rocky Mountains.

_____ The Lewis and Clark Expedition reaches the Pacific Ocean.

_____ Jefferson chooses Lewis to head an exploring mission.

_____ The Lewis and Clark expedition sets off up the Missouri River.

_____ Jefferson buys the land of the Louisiana Purchase from the French.

_____ Lewis and Clark meet Sacajawea at Fort Mandan in North Dakota.

_____ The expedition crosses the Rocky Mountains on Shoshone horses.

USING PRIMARY SOURCES

We know about Sacajawea from Lewis and Clark's journals of the trip.

On May 14, 1805, one of the expedition's boats nearly capsized on the Missouri River. Clark wrote that among the items nearly lost were:

> "our papers, instruments, books, medicine . . . in short almost every article indispensably necessary . . . the articles which floated out was nearly all caught by [Sacajawea]."

Jan. 6, 1806, after the group had reached the Pacific Ocean, Lewis wrote that "[Sacajawea] had traveled a long way to see the great waters, and now that monstrous fish [whale] was also to be seen, she thought it very hard she could not be permitted to see either."

These two incidents reveal that Sacajawea was

    a. timid and quiet.

    b. quick thinking and curious.

    c. moody and disobedient.

WRITE ABOUT IT

The explorers did take Sacajawea with them to view the Pacific Ocean and the remains of the whale. Imagine that you are Sacajawea and you are writing about your first visit to the "great waters." In your history journal, write about what you see.

AN ORATOR IN A RED JACKET SPEAKS
THE GREAT TEKAMTHI, ALSO CALLED TECUMSEH
OSEOLA

SUMMARY *Iroquois chief Sagoyewatha spoke eloquently on behalf of his people. Shawnee chief Tecumseh tried to unite all Indian tribes against the white settlers who were invading their land. When he was a boy, Osceola witnessed a fierce civil war pitting Creeks who wanted to adopt a white way of life against those who did not.*

ACCESS

Tecumseh tried to stem the tide of white migration westward but white power was simply too great. Copy the sequence of events chart from page 9. In each box, list an event in Tecumseh's life that led to the next event and finally to his death.

WORD BANK   orator   shaman   prophet   incorporate

Choose words from the Word Bank to complete the sentences. One word is not used at all.

Shawnee warrior Tecumseh traveled around the country urging Indian tribes to

_____ into a mighty league. His brother Tenskwatawa, who was also called the

_____, was a religious leader, or _____, who urged the Shawnee to give

up white ways.

WORD PLAY

Look up the word you did not use and write the word in a sentence.

_____

What verb has the same root?

_____

COMPARE AND CONTRAST

These phrases describe three American Indian leaders from the early 19th century. Sort the phrases into three columns, "Sagoyewatha," "Tecumseh," and "Oseola," in the graphic organizer on the next page.

Tried to unite all Indian tribes

His people were defeated by Andrew Jackson

A great orator

An Iroquois

Fought for the British

His name means "He Causes Them To Be Awake"

A Creek

A Shawnee

His people were defeated by William Henry Harrison

Brother to the Prophet

Lived with the Seminoles

Sagoyewatha	Tecumseh	Oseola

USING PRIMARY SOURCES

In 1810, Tecumseh spoke before William Henry Harrison, governor of the Indiana Territory:

> "You are continually driving the red people [from their land], when at last you will drive them into the [ocean] where they can't either stand or work. Brother, you ought to know what you are doing with the Indians. . . . It is a very bad thing and we do not like it."

WRITE ABOUT IT

IDENTIFYING POINT OF VIEW

An editorial is an article that expresses an opinion. With a parent or partner, find an editorial in a local newspaper. Then, in your history journal, write an editorial from the viewpoint of Tecumseh. You are trying to convince white officials like William Henry Harrison that driving Indians off their land is the wrong thing to do. What do you say?

Now write an editorial from Harrison's point of view. How would he defend the actions of the white settlers?

THE REVOLUTIONARY WAR PART II, OR THE WAR OF 1812

SUMMARY *The War of 1812 convinced the world that the United States could hold its own against the greatest army and navy on earth.*

ACCESS

The war of 1812 actually took place between 1812 and 1815. In your history journal, copy the Timeline found on page 9. Label the dates 1812, 1813, 1814, and 1815. Then fill in the event boxes with the following events: "The U.S. declares war"; "British invade Washington, D.C."; "British bombard Fort McHenry"; "Andrew Jackson wins Battle of New Orleans"; "peace treaty signed."

WORD BANK   anthem   rockets   perilous   ramparts   foe

Choose words from the Word Bank to complete the sentences. One word is not used at all.

1. The _____ marched into Washington, D.C., and set fire to the Capitol and

the President's House.

2. Throughout the night, Francis Scott Key could see the fiery _____ bursting

over Fort McHenry.

3. The attackers climbed over the _____ of the fort.

4. "The Star-Spangled Banner" is the national _____ of the United States.

WORD PLAY

Look up the word you did not use in the dictionary and write it in a sentence.

_____

What shorter word can you make from this word? _____

CRITICAL THINKING

CAUSE AND EFFECT

Draw a line from each cause and connect it to the correct result, or effect. Then read the matched pairs aloud to a parent or partner.

CAUSE

The British captured American ships and sailors

The War Hawks wanted to go to war against Great Britain.

The British won the war against Napoleon

The British marched into Washington, D.C.,

Merchants sank their own ships in Baltimore Harbor

Francis Scott Key saw the flag still waving over Fort McHenry

No one knew the peace treaty ending the war had already been signed

After the war the President's House was painted white to cover the burn marks

EFFECT

SO he wrote "The Star-Spangled Banner."

SO James and Dolley Madison had to flee the capital.

SO it was renamed the White House.

SO Americans were angry at the British.

SO Andrew Jackson fought the British at New Orleans

SO British ships couldn't sail into the city.

SO the British were able to send more soldiers to America.

SO they convinced President Madison to declare war.

IN YOUR OWN WORDS

You've probably sung "The Star-Spangled Banner" a hundred times. But what does it mean? Read the song on page 83. Then, in your history journal, rewrite the verses in your own words. Look up any words you don't understand in the dictionary.

YANKEE INGENUITY: COTTON AND MUSKETS

SUMMARY *The Industrial Revolution transformed the lives of Americans in both North and South.*

ACCESS

How did the invention of machines change the way ordinary people lived in the 19th century? In your history journal, copy the "K-W-L" chart from page 8. In the first column, write everything you already know about the Industrial Revolution. In the middle column, write down any questions you have. As you read the next few chapters, write everything that you learn in the third column.

WORD BANK   market revolution   market economy   farm economy

Choose words from the Word Bank to complete the sentences.

1. In a _____, people grow or make most of what they need.

2. In a _____, people earn the money to buy what they need

3. The 19th century change from a farm economy to a market economy is called the

_____.

CRITICAL THINKING

CLASSIFICATION

The Industrial Revolution changed the lives of workers and non-workers alike. The sentences below describe both advantages and disadvantages of the factory system. in your history journal, make a 2-column chart labeled "Advantages" and "Disadvantages." Put the sentences in the correct columns.

Housewives were freed from
   spinning yarn and making cloth.

Ordinary people could buy manufactured goods.

Children worked long hours in the factories.

Factories caused air and water pollution.

Factory goods cost less than handmade goods.

Workers were injured in factories

Skilled craftsmen lost their living.

The United States became more productive.

Factory work is boring and repetitive.

People started wearing more cotton.

USING PRIMARY SOURCES

A New England Girlhood 1889

Lucy Larcom went to work in a factory when she was eleven years old. Later she wrote a memoir about her experiences.

> The last window in the row behind me was filled with flourishing houseplants . . . fragrant-leaved geraniums. . . . Standing before that window, I could look across the room and see girls moving backwards and forwards among the spinning-frames, sometimes stopping, sometimes reaching up their arms . . . with easy and not ungraceful movements. On the whole, it was far from being a disagreeable place to stay in.

1. Why do you suppose Lucy has chosen a spot by the window?

2. Circle two words that tell you why Lucy liked the flowers.

3. From Lucy's viewpoint, it looks as if the other girls are

   a. dancing.   b. running.   c. praying.   d. crying

4. How do you think Lucy feels about her job?

   a. She loves it.   b. She hates it.   c. She is bored by it.   d. She doesn't mind it.

WRITE ABOUT IT

Imagine that you are working in a New England textile mill in the 1830s. In your history journal, write a diary entry about a typical day in your life. When do you wake up and go to work? When do you go home? What do you eat? What do you do on the job? Write down a conversation you have with another child in the mill.

GOING PLACES

SUMMARY *New roads and canals quickly and cheaply transported goods and people from place to place.*

ACCESS

Working songs like "Erie Canal" helped workers pass the time while they worked. With a parent or partner, find a recording of "Erie Canal" on the Internet or in the library. Listen to the song. What do you think the laborers were doing as they sang this song?

WORD BANK   corduroy   pike   aqueduct   toll   towpaths   camber   lock   flatboat   macadam

Choose words from the Word Bank to complete the paragraph. One word is not used at all.

Early 19th-century America witnessed a transportation revolution. Wooden _____

roads were replaced by _____ roads of crushed rock and tar. The slope, or

_____, of the roads ensured that water would run off into drainage ditches. To pay

for some of the roads, private companies installed _____ across the entrances. After

travelers paid a fare, or _____, a gatekeeper would lift the pike and let the travelers on

the road. Also, canals were built to transport passenger boats and _____ from

one natural waterway the next. The boats were pulled by horses and mules that walked on

_____ beside the canals. _____ would raise or lower boats from

one level to the next.

WORD PLAY

Look the word you did not use up in a dictionary and write it in a sentence.

_____

CRITICAL THINKING

MAIN IDEA AND SUPPORTING DETAILS

Each sentence in italics below states a main idea from the chapter. Put a check mark in the blanks in front of all of the sentences that support or tell more about the main idea.

1. *New roads made it easier for Americans to travel, and to buy and sell goods.*

___ a. Vans stuffed with cotton traveled north on the National Road.

___ b. The National Road was paid for by the federal government.

__ c. Emigrants used paved roads to head west.

2. *[The Erie Canal] was a manmade river, it was an engineering marvel!*

   __ a. The canal ran 350 miles from Albany to Buffalo.

   __ b. Towns grew up along the canal.

   __ c. The Erie Canal had 83 locks and 18 aqueducts.

USING PRIMARY SOURCES

In 1840, Virginian John Parsons traveled from Cumberland, Maryland, to Wheeling West Virginia, on the National Road:

> A broad white highway, winding ribbonlike over mountain top and through a valley, with its many stately stone bridges, its iron mile posts and its great iron toll gates, and over it the long procession of stage coaches, like ours, going and coming . . . the great Conestoga wagons . . . long and deep . . . the lower broadside painted blue, with a movable board inserted above painted red, the covering of white canvas . . . the emigrant wagon, whose occupants [camped] nightly by the roadside; an occasional young man on horseback with a country lass behind him. . . . and now and again a long line of Negro slaves . . . fastened to a long thick rope.

1. Name five different kinds of travelers on the National Road

_____

2. Name the kind of transportation each group uses.

_____

WRITE ABOUT IT

Imagine that you are traveling on the National Road early in the 19th century. What type of transportation would you choose? Write a letter to a friend describing your experiences.

TEAKETTLE POWER

SUMMARY *American and British inventors figured out ways to harness steampower to drive steamboats and trains*

ACCESS

People like Robert Fulton and Peter Cooper made inventions that changed people's lives. In your history journal, copy the main idea map graphic organizer from page 8. In the largest circle, write the word "Inventors." In the smaller circles, write words that describe an inventor. Match each quality with a person you read about in The New Nation.

WORD BANK   iron horse   horsepower   steampower   steamboats

Choose words from the Word Bank to complete the sentences. One word is not used at all.

1. Before the steam locomotive, _____ was used to pull railcars along tracks.

2. An early term for a locomotive was a _____.

3. Inventor Robert Fulton designed a _____ that traveled from New York City to Albany in only 32 hours.

WORD PLAY

Write the word you did not use in a sentence.

_____

CRITICAL THINKING

ALL OVER THE MAP

Look at the map of Roads and Rails, Canals and Trails circa 1840 on pages 122-123 and answer the following questions:

1. Your boat travels up the Hudson River from New York City. Name ten rivers and lakes you can

   reach using canals and natural waterways.

   _____

   _____

   _____

2. Where are most of the railway lines? _____

   Why? _____

3. This map does not distinguish between roads and trails. What do you think the difference

   between them is?

   _____

4. Look up the word "circa" in the dictionary. What does it mean?

_____

5. Find the section on abbreviations in your dictionary. What is the abbreviation for

"circa"?_____

USING PRIMARY SOURCES

Reread the passage written by Charles Dickens on page 121. Then answer the following questions.

1. To what imaginary creature does Dickens compare the train?

_____

2. What words does he use to describe the sounds that the train makes?

_____

_____

3. How do people react when the train pulls into town?

_____

3. Why is the "monster" thirsty? _____

What does it need to drink? _____

MAKING WORDS
A TIME TO WEEP

SUMMARY *Sequoyah invented a written Cherokee alphabet and gave his people a new way to communicate. Even though the Supreme Court ruled Indian removal unconstitutional, President Andrew Jackson sent the Cherokees west on the Trail of Tears.*

ACCESS

Have you ever heard of the Trail of Tears? In your history journal, copy the "K-W-L" chart from page 8. In the first column, write everything you already know about the forced removal of Indians from their land. In the middle column, write down any questions you have. As you read these two chapters, write everything that you learn in the third column.

WORD BANK   versus   opinion   compensation

Choose words from the Word Bank to complete the sentences.

1. A judge's written commentary on a case is called a _____.

2. _____ means "against."

3. Territory west of the Mississippi was no _____ for the Cherokees' loss of their homeland.

CRITICAL THINKING

SEQUENCE OF EVENTS

The sentences below list events in the history of the Cherokees. Use numbers to put them in the correct order (use "1" for the first event, and so on).

_____The Cherokees printed their own newspaper.

_____One out of four Cherokees died on the Trail of Tears.

_____The Cherokees appealed their case to the Supreme Court.

_____Congress passed the Indian Removal Act in 1830.

_____Andrew Jackson ignored the Supreme Court decision.

_____Gold was discovered on Cherokee land.

_____Sequoyah invented the Cherokee alphabet.

_____Chief Justice John Marshall ruled that the Cherokees had the right to their own land.

USING PRIMARY SOURCES

Read the sidebar on page 129 about the Trail of Tears. Who are the "hungry wolves" who "follow in the train of the captors"?

Now read this passage by William Shorey Coodey, who witnessed the beginning of the first forced march of the Cherokees:

> At length the word was given to "move on." I glanced along the line and the form of Going Snake, an aged and respected chief whose head eighty winters had whitened, mounted on his favorite pony passed before me and led the way in advance, followed by a number of young men on horse back. At this very moment a low sound of distant thunder fell on my ear. . . . I almost fancied a voice of divine indignation for the wrongs of my poor and unhappy countrymen, driven by brutal power from all they loved and cherished in the land of their fathers, to gratify the cravings of [greed].

1. What is Coodey's opinion of the forced march?

2. What does he think the thunder might mean?

3. Why does he think the Cherokees are being forced to leave their homeland?

WRITE ABOUT IT

The Trail of Tears is an example of injustice, or unfairness. In your history journal, write about an injustice that you have witnessed or read about.

CHAPTER 30 31

THE KING AND HIS PEOPLE
ABOLITIONISTS WANT TO END SLAVERY

SUMMARY *"King Cotton" ruled the South after the invention of the cotton gin and guaranteed the continuation of slavery. Northern abolitionists alarmed southern slave owners by demanding an end to slavery.*

ACCESS

The Cotton Kingdom stretched from the Atlantic Ocean to Texas. In your history journal, copy the main idea map graphic organizer from page 8. In the largest circle, write "King Cotton's People." In each of the smaller circles, write the names of different types of people in the South and a few facts about each.

WORD BANK   abolitionist   moral   immoral   secede   lynch

Choose words from the Word Bank to complete the sentences. One word is not used at all

1. George Washington and Robert E. Lee both felt that slavery was _____.

2. To _____ means to execute without a lawful trial.

3. Some southerners argued that the southern states should _____ from the Union

    and form their own country.

4. William Lloyd Garrison was the most famous white _____.

WORD PLAY

Look up the word you did not use in the dictionary and use it in a sentence.

_____

What other words have the same root?

_____

CRITICAL THINKING

CAUSE AND EFFECT Match the effect in the left column with the correct cause in the right column. Write them as sentences connected with "because." There is one extra cause.

EFFECT	CAUSE
The African slave trade became unlawful	The Southern economy depended on slavery.
Growing cotton became very profitable	Eli Whitney invented the cotton gin.
Slavery flourished in southern states and territories	Abolitionist presses were destroyed.
The South did not want to abolish slavery	Newcomers could not compete with slaves for jobs.
Immigrants did not settle in the South	Planters needed slaves to pick cotton.
Congress passed the Missouri Compromise in 1820	They hated slavery.
Southern states passed stricter laws governing slaves	The Constitution said trade would end in 1808.
Abolitionists published newspapers and books that attacked slavery	Some slaves rebelled against their white owners.
	To balance the number of slave and free states.

USING PRIMARY SOURCES

Compare the quotations from William Lloyd Garrison and Frederick Douglass in the sidebar on page 156.

1. What words would you use to describe the tone of both passages?

   a. happy and content

   b. sad and hopeless

   c. excited and determined

2. In the Garrison passage, "moderation" means

   a. "restraint."

   b. "anger."

3. What does Douglass mean when he says that *The Liberator* became his "meat and drink"?

4. Which of Douglass's words reveal that he too has been a slave?

WRITE ABOUT IT

Imagine that you are writing an editorial in an abolitionist newspaper. In your history journal, write the argument from the point of view of a white abolitionist. What would your headline be? What argument would you make to free the slaves? Then, write the argument from the viewpoint of an escaped slave. How would your argument change?

CHAPTER 32

FREDERICK DOUGLASS

SUMMARY *Frederick Douglass escaped from slavery and became an important abolitionist.*

ACCESS

Frederick Douglass was a brilliant spokesman for freedom and civil rights both before and after the Civil War. In your history journal, copy the main idea map graphic organizer from page 8. In the largest circle put Douglass's name. In the smaller circles write facts that you learn about Douglass as you read the chapter.

WORD BANK   slave catcher   dextrous   bigotry   freeman

Choose words from the Word Bank to complete the sentences. One word is not used at all

1. After Douglass escaped to the North, he became a _____.

2. Even after Douglass was living in Massachusetts, he knew that he could still be captured by a _____.

3. All his life, Douglass spoke out against injustice and _____.

WORD PLAY

Look up the word you did not use and write it in a sentence.

_____

CRITICAL THINKING

SEQUENCE OF EVENTS

The sentences below describe events in Frederick Douglass's life. Write "before" or "after" in the blank to complete each sentence correctly.

1. Young Frederick was sent to Baltimore _____ his mother died.

2. Frederick's new mistress tried to teach him to read _____ her husband ordered her not to.

3. Frederick's white friends helped him to read _____ Frederick traded food for lessons.

4. Douglass's new master used to whip him _____ Douglass decided that some day he would be free.

5. Douglass became an antislavery speaker _____ he escaped to Massachusetts.

6. Douglass started an abolitionist newspaper _____ he wrote *Narrative of the Life of Frederick Douglass*.

7. Douglass became an advisor to Abraham Lincoln _____ Lincoln became president.

USING PRIMARY SOURCES

COMPREHENSION

Narrative of the Life of Frederick Douglas   1845

In his *Narrative*, Douglass described his state of mind immediate after he had escaped to the North.

> I have frequently been asked how I felt when I found myself in a free state . . . I suppose I felt as one may imagine the unarmed mariner to feel when he is rescued by a friendly man-of-war from the pursuit of a pirate . . . [or] one who had escaped a den of hungry lions. . . . But the loneliness overcame me. There I was in the midst of thousands, and yet a perfect stranger. . . . I was afraid to speak to any one for fear of speaking to the wrong one, and thereby falling into the hands of money-loving kidnappers.

1. "Marine" means "of or relating to the sea." What do you think "mariner" means?

2. To what does Douglass compare slave owners? Circle the two comparisons.

3. What two conflicting emotions does Douglass feel?

   a. relief and fear

   b. sorrow and gladness

   c. love and hatred

WRITE ABOUT IT

Imagine that you are Frederick Douglass and you have just escaped from slavery. You want to express the way you feel. In your history journal, write a seven-line poem with each line starting with a letter in the word F-R-E-E-D-O-M.

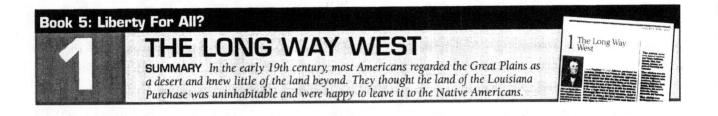

1 THE LONG WAY WEST

SUMMARY *In the early 19th century, most Americans regarded the Great Plains as a desert and knew little of the land beyond. They thought the land of the Louisiana Purchase was uninhabitable and were happy to leave it to the Native Americans.*

ACCESS

This chapter explains some of the first impressions of explorers who traveled across the Great Plains. A good graphic organizer for this chapter is the main idea map on page 8. Copy the diagram in your history journal. In the largest circle, write the words "Great American Desert." Use each of the webs to write facts about this "desert" that you read in the chapter.

WHAT DO YOU KNOW? What is the longest trip you have ever taken? How did you travel? Did you take photographs on the trip? Why or why not? Why do you think many people take cameras when they travel? What do you think travelers or explorers used before cameras?

WORD BANK   iron horse   Great American Desert   prickly pear   bluff

Complete the sentences below with words from Word Bank. One word is not used.

1. The _____ was the original term used to describe the area we know as the

   Great Plains.

2. A _____ is the fruit of a certain type of cactus.

3. Indians used the term _____ to describe the trains that crossed their

   lands.

WORD PLAY

In a dictionary, look up both definitions of the word that was not used. Write two sentences using to the two different definitions.

_____

_____

CRITICAL THINKING

MAIN IDEA AND SUPPORTING DETAILS

Each sentence in italics below states a main idea from the chapter. Put a check mark in the blank in front of the ONE sentence that DOES NOT support or tell more about the main idea.

1. *When President Thomas Jefferson purchased the Louisiana Territory from France, in 1803, a few people grumbled, but most people approved.*

   _____ a. Britain claimed Oregon, though there was some dispute about that.

   _____ b. Hardly anyone liked the idea of France having land on the border of the United States, or of France controlling the port of New Orleans.

   _____ c. It was a huge hunk of land that went from the Mississippi River to the Rocky Mountains.

2. *Early in the 19th century, most people in the United States thought there was plenty of room for the Indians on land to the west of the Mississippi.*

_____ a. And, at first, the Indians were friendly toward the newcomers.

_____ b. But most Europeans and Americans talked of Indians as "savages," and they usually acted as if those savages had no rights.

_____ c. Besides, few Americans seemed to have any desire to live in the Louisiana Territory.

3. *This was fertile land, but Easterners didn't know it.*

_____ a. None of the members of the expedition seemed particularly impressed with what they found.

_____ b. They were used to chopping down trees to make farmland.

_____ c. People listened to Long, and for the next 20 years, most travelers who ventured west agreed: The Great Plains was an uninhabitable desert.

WORKING WITH PRIMARY SOURCES

Read the words of Stephen Long below. Answer the questions that follow.

> In regard to this extensive section of the country . . . it is . . . unfit for cultivation, and . . . uninhabitable by a people depending on agriculture for . . . subsistence.

1. In the statement, what does "extensive section" mean?

_____ a. Valuable land   _____ b. large area   _____ c. private property

2. What does "unfit for cultivation" mean?

_____ a. polluted   _____ b. not for sale   _____ c. unsuited for plowing

3. Who are the people "depending on agriculture"?

_____ a. Americans   _____ b. explorers   _____ c. Indians

WRITING

Study the painting and caption on page 14. Imagine that it is 1820 and you are going to send the painting back to friends. Write a three-sentence "postcard message" to accompany the painting.

_____

_____

MOUNTAIN MEN

CHAPTER 2

SUMMARY *A group of rough-and-tumble fur traders known as mountain men took the lead in blazing trails across Native American lands west of the Mississippi River.*

ACCESS

This chapter discusses important explorers in the early 1800s. In your history journal, make a cause and effect chart like the one on page 9. For the first cause, write "William Ashley advertised for mountain men." List the effect. What was the cause that resulted from the first effect? Fill in at least five cause-and-effect relationships.

WITH PARENT OR PARTNER Study the map of the Expeditions of Jedediah Smith on page 18. Try to locate approximately where your area of California is on the map. Did Smith pass through that area? What number on the map is closest to your community? What cities on the map are still found in California today?

WORD BANK   rendezvous   mountain man   trekked   petrified   massacre

Complete the sentences below with words from Word Bank. One word is not used.

1. Setting out to trap beaver, a _____ traveled alone as he hiked, or _____, across the west.

2. Each year the mountain men met in a get-together called a _____.

3. Trees that have turned to stone over millions of years are said to be _____, which is also a word meaning "frightened."

WORD PLAY

In a dictionary, look up both definitions of the word that was not used. How does the first syllable help to explain the meaning of the word? _____

CRITICAL THINKING

FACT OR OPINION

A fact is a statement that can be proven. An opinion judges things or people, but cannot be proved or disproved. Put F or O in front of the sentences below from the chapter.

_____ 1. The ad in the St. Louis newspaper, in February 1822, called for men willing to try something new.

_____ 2. Some people like dangers, some like to be free of civilization, and some like to live by their wits.

_____ 3. If only Daniel Boone had been around—he died in 1820 at age 86—Boone would have loved being one of Ashley's Mountain Men.

_____ 4. It was Smith who found the South Pass, a gap through the Rockies in the Wyoming region.

_____ 5. Jedediah was just getting started as a mountain man when he survived his first Indian massacre.

_____ 6. But, like most of the mountain men, Beckwourth was restless.

_____ 7. Once, sitting around a campfire, an army officer told Bridger a story from Shakespeare.

PRIMARY SOURCES

Read the words of Jedediah Smith below. Answer the questions that follow.

> I traverse the mountains covered with eternal snow . . . I am . . . satisfied if I can gather a few roots, a few snails , . . or a piece of horse flesh, or a . . . roasted dog.

1. What does "traverse" mean in the excerpt above?

    ___ a. carry   ____ b. cross   _____ c. ski

2. Why does Smith call the snow "eternal"?

    ____ a. It never melts.   _____ b. It is white.   _____ c. It is cold.

3. Which of the food items described are wild?

    _____

4. When would a mountain man be most likely to eat an animal that was a companion?

    _____

WRITING

Imagine that you are the mountain man who sewed Smith's ear and scalp back on after the grizzly attack. Write a short diary entry in your history journal describing the sights and sounds of the procedures. What tools did you use? What did you use as thread?

CHAPTER 3 4

RIDING THE TRAIL TO SANTA FE
SUSAN MAGOFFIN'S DIARY

SUMMARY *U.S explorers also found their way into lands claimed by Mexico. The lure of profit led them to carve out a trail to Santa Fe, paving the way for the later U.S. takeover of New Mexico. Susan Magoffin was among the "foreign invaders" who traveled into Spanish-speaking New Mexico. Her brother James helped in the bloodless U.S. takeover of the Mexican territory.*

ACCESS

To help understand the importance of the Santa Fe Trail in the exploration of the southwest that is described in these chapters, make a K-W-L chart in your history journal like the one on page 8. In the "What I Know" column write what you know about the Santa Fe Trail (if you don't know anything that's OK). In the "What I Want to Know" column, write five questions you have about the trail. After you read the chapter, fill out the "What I Learned" column with answers to your questions and other information.

WITH A PARENT OR PARTNER Study the map on page 23. Using the scale miles determine how much longer the Mountain Route was than the Cimarron Cutoff. Which route required travelers to cross more rivers? Compare the map to a modern map. What states did the Santa Fe Trail pass through? What do you think is the name of river that is unmarked just above "Mexico" on the map on page 23?

WORD BANK   pinnacle   rawhide   Santa Fe Trail   blight   Great Potato Famine   poor law   mission

Complete the sentences below with words from Word Bank above. One word is not used.

1. The _____ is the highest point on a mountain.

2. A _____ or plant disease, caused the

   _____ in Ireland.

3. Starvation and a _____ that taxed peasants more than wealthy

   people caused a wave of migration from Ireland to the United States in the 1840s.

4. The _____ was the main route southwest from Missouri to Mexico

5. Instead of rope, many travelers used the skin of cattle called _____.

WORD PLAY

The word that is not used has two meanings. You can figure out one meaning by looking at the map on page 23. The other use of the word is on page 28. Write two sentences using the different meanings.

_____

_____

CRITICAL THINKING

SEQUENCE OF EVENTS The sentences below describe the events in the opening of the Santa Fe Trail. Put 1, 2, 3, and so on in front of the sentences that describe what happened.

_____ Susan Magoffin headed west from Missouri.

_____ William Becknell led four men west "for the purpose of trading."

_____ Josiah Gregg went west with 100 wagons.

_____ That year, 5,000 freight wagons headed west from Missouri.

_____ Zebulon Pike tried to climb a mountain that was later named after him.

_____ Becknell went back with $3000 worth of trade goods.

WORKING WITH PRIMARY SOURCES

Read the words from Susan Magoffin's diary. Answer the questions that follow.

> A parcel of Indians are . . . peeping in at me . . . It is a novel sight for them . . . the . . . descendants of the original inhabitants . . . cultivators of the soil.

1. What does the word "parcel" mean above? _____ a. package _____ b. present _____ c. group

2. What does the word "novel" mean above?_____ a. book _____ b. new _____ c. unpleasant

3. How might you determine that the Indians are shy and curious?

_____

4. Review Long's comments about the Plains from Chapter 1. How does his opinion differ from

   Susan Magoffin's? _____

WRITING

Study the drawing of the river crossing on page 27. In your history journal, write a diary entry that evening describing the difficulties and dangers of crossing a river in a wagon. Use some of the information from Susan Magoffin that is given in the caption.

PIONEERS: TAKING THE TRAIL WEST
GETTING THERE

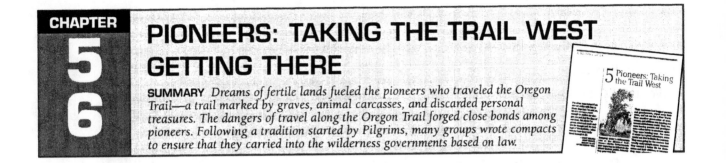

SUMMARY *Dreams of fertile lands fueled the pioneers who traveled the Oregon Trail—a trail marked by graves, animal carcasses, and discarded personal treasures. The dangers of travel along the Oregon Trail forged close bonds among pioneers. Following a tradition started by Pilgrims, many groups wrote compacts to ensure that they carried into the wilderness governments based on law.*

ACCESS

These chapters describe the journey west of American settlers on the Oregon Trail. A good graphic organizer for this chapter is the main idea map on page 8. Copy the diagram in your history journal. In the largest circle, write the words "Traveling West." Use each of the webs to write about the challenges these pioneers faced, such as water, heat, food, and other topics. Fill in the circles with facts as you read them.

WHAT DO YOU KNOW? Suppose you were going on a six month trip and could only take one big duffel bag of personal belongings—including clothes. What would you take? Suppose you had to walk for most of this trip and the weather could change from warm and sunny to cold and snowy in minutes. How would that change what you would take? Make a list. Share it with your classmates.

WORD BANK   prairie schooner   emigrant   pioneer   wagon train   Humboldt sink   cholera

Complete the sentences below with words from Word Bank above. One word is not used.

1. An _____ who left the east to travel west was also called _____.

2. The _____, the main vehicle for traveling west, was named after a two-masted boat.

3. These "boats" usually traveled in a long line, which was called a _____ after

   another form of transportation.

4. Travelers who decided to go to California were often dismayed to arrive at the

   _____, where an important river suddenly ended in a desert.

In a dictionary, look up the word that was not used. Rewrite the sentence in the chapter in which

the word appears, using the definition.

CRITICAL THINKING

DRAWING CONCLUSIONS Each sentence below is taken from the words of a pioneer in the chapters. Put a check in front of all of the conclusions that can be drawn from each statement.

1. A good many wagons are left at this point [Fort Laramie] many coming to the conclusion of getting along without them.

   _____ a. Pioneers often took more belongings than they needed.

_____ b. Pioneers often arrived in Oregon with very few possessions.

_____ c. Pioneers returned for the items they left behind.

2. We did not have sense enough to realize our danger; we just had the time of our lives.

_____ a. Traveling across the country was often exciting.

_____ b. Children did nothing but play on the journey.

_____ c. Dangers were often hidden on the trail.

3. At this place, however, there are Indians who swim the river from morning to night. There is many a drove of cattle that could not be got over without their help.

_____ a. Indians often helped pioneers on the journey west.

_____ b. Pioneers did not always fear Indians.

_____ c. There was no violence between Indians and pioneers.

4. It has been a prosperous day; more than twenty miles have been accomplished.

_____ a. "Prosperous" means that the wagon train earned money.

_____ b. "Prosperous" means that the wagon train covered a good distance.

_____ c. Twenty miles was a long distance for a wagon to travel in a day.

MAP

Study the map on page 41. Answer the questions that follow.

1. The Missouri River and North Platte River joined at

_____ a. St. Louis. ___ b. Independence. ___ c. Council Bluffs.

2. Wagon trains that left Independence, Missouri, traveled along the banks of which rivers?

___ a. Missouri and North Platte ___ b. North Platte and Snake ___ c. Missouri and Mississippi

3. Wagon trains split off to go to Oregon or California after they crossed

___ a. the Snake River. _____ b. the North Platte River. ___ c. South Pass.

4. What kind of bird is shown on the map? _____

   Why is it shown? _____

WRITING

Review all of the diary entries in the chapters. Try to imagine life crossing the country from Missouri to Oregon. In your history journal, write a diary entry on a clear starlit night as you sit around a campfire. How far did the wagon trail travel? What animals did you see? Was it hot or cool? Were there any accidents? What did you have for meals? What sounds do you hear?

LATTER-DAY SAINTS

SUMMARY *The Mormons were pioneers in search of religious freedom. Their settlement of the Utah territory increased the culture pluralism of our country.*

ACCESS

This chapter discusses the challenges faced by Mormons before and during their migration to Utah. In your history journal, make a cause and effect chart like the one on page 9. For the first cause, write "Joseph Smith leads followers to Nauvoo." List the effect. What was the cause that resulted from the first effect? Fill in at least five cause-and-effect relationships.

WITH A PARENT OR PARTNER Study the map on page 45. How many of the states that are shown within borders can you name? Where is the Mississippi River? Compare the map to the map on page 41. Where would St. Louis be located on this map? Where is the Missouri River? The North Platte? Where is South Pass?

WORD BANK   Latter-Day Saints   Mormons   utopian   polygamy   pluralism   bigots

Complete the sentences below with words from Word Bank above. One word is not used.

1. Joseph Smith's followers, who called themselves _____, were known as _____ to most people.

2. Smith dreamed of building a _____ community, where people put aside personal goals for the common good.

3. Many people objected to the Mormon practice of _____ in which men had more than one wife.

4. _____, or many-sidedness, is an American ideal that is sometimes difficult for people to accept.

CRITICAL THINKING

FACT OR OPINION

A fact is a statement that can be proven. An opinion judges things or people, but cannot be proved or disproved. Put F or O in front of the sentences below from the chapter.

_____ 1. Like the Pilgrims and Puritans, they called themselves "Saints."

_____ 2. The name of their church was too long for most people to bother saying.

_____ 3. The First Amendment to the Constitution forbids religious persecution.

_____ 4. In 1845, Young sent a few Mormons west to check out the Great Salt Lake.

_____ 5. It wasn't easy crossing the treeless plains, or climbing into the mountains.

_____ 6. His may have been the best organized of all the western treks.

_____ 7. When Brigham Young died in 1877, there were 140,000 Mormons living in the Utah territory in 325 towns.

PRIMARY SOURCES

Read the words of the resolution passed in Warsaw, Illinois, in 1844. Answer the questions that follow.

> The adherents of Smith, as a body, should be driven . . . into Nauvoo . . . a war of extermination should be waged, to the entire destruction . . . of his adherents.

1. Another word for "adherents" is

_____ a. wives.   _____ b. followers.   _____ c. enemies.

2. Another way to say "as a body" is

_____ a. "Smith's family."   _____ b. "men, women, and children."   _____ c. "corpses."

3. What is a "war of extermination"?

_____

WRITING

In your history journal, write a letter to editor of the *Warsaw Times* that explains your feeling about the resolution. Do you agree? Why? Do you disagree? Why?

COAST-TO-COAST DESTINY

SUMMARY *The idea of manifest destiny was fueled by the writing of California traveler Richard Henry Dana. President James Polk began diplomatic probes to wrest this land from the Mexicans.*

ACCESS

This chapter talks about the idea that Americans had a right to settle anywhere they wished, including in land claimed by another country. To organize the information, copy the outline graphic organizer from page 8 into your history journal. For the main idea, write "Manifest Destiny." For topics put "Leaders," "Land," and "Settlement." Put at least two points under each topic.

WHAT DO YOU KNOW? Does your town or city have a Spanish name? What other locations in your region have Spanish names? Make a list of all the Spanish words that name locations and then translate those names into English.

WORD BANK   manifest destiny   rancheros   lasso

Complete the sentences below with words from Word Bank. One word is not used.

1. Many Americans believed that it was _____ for the United States to extend from coast to coast.

2. The _____, wealthy landowners in California, did not like Americans coming into their territory in large numbers.

Read page 51 to find the word that is not used. Use the word in a sentence as a noun. Then use it in a sentence as a verb

_____

_____

CRITICAL THINKING

MAIN IDEA AND SUPPORTING DETAILS Each sentences in italics below states a main idea from the chapter. Put a check mark in the blanks in front of the ONE sentence that DOES NOT support or tell more about the main idea.

1. *President James K. Polk wanted California and Oregon, and so did most other Americans.*

   ___ a. Indians had lived in California for thousands of years, cut off from the rest of the world.

   ___ b. The land was enticing, and there was something that convinced people that it was right to take it.

   ___ c. It was an idea called "Manifest Destiny."

2. *Both Great Britain and the United States claimed Oregon.*

   ___ a. In 1846, President Polk signed a treaty with England: the Oregon Treaty.

   ___ b. The two nations agreed to split the Oregon territory on the 49th parallel.

   ___ c. California belonged to Mexico.

3. The priests built Catholic missions along the coast.

    ____ a. The priests believed they were serving God by baptizing and teaching Native Americans.

    ____ b. When Mexico won its independence from Spain in 1821, Mexicans became rulers of California.

    ____ c. They planned, they said, to give the missions to the Indians.

PRIMARY SOURCES

Read Dana's description of California. Answer the questions that follow.

> The soil is as rich as a man could wish; climate as good as any in the world; water abundant, and situation extremely beautiful.

1. Who would be happiest if soil was "rich"?

    ____ a. miners   ____ b. soldiers   ____ c. farmers

2. What is another word that means about the same as "abundant"?

    ____ a. rare   ____ b. limited   ____ c. plentiful

3. What does the word "situation" mean in the sentence above?

    ____ a. place   ____ b. jobs   ____ c. problem

WRITING

Write one or two sentences describing California in your own words. Mention the aspects that Dana mentions: soil, climate, and water. Express your opinion.

_____

_____

CHAPTER 9

A HERO OF HIS TIMES

SUMMARY *John Frémont played a key role in securing California for America. He first created interest in the territory and then, in a controversial manner, helped America claim it.*

ACCESS

This chapter covers a number of events in the life of John Charles Frémont. To help organize the information make a timeline graphic organizer like the one on page 9. Each time you read a date in the chapter, write it in the left column. In the right column, list the event that took place.

WHAT DO YOU KNOW? What does the word hero mean to you? Who is a personal hero to you? Why would explorers have been heroes to Americans in the 1840s?

WORD BANK   latitude   longitude   topographical   Great Basin   elite

Complete the sentences below with words from Word Bank. One word is not used

1. The _____, a desert region in Nevada, was a land of shimmering lakes in

   prehistoric times.

2. A _____ map shows the shape of landscapes rather than borders.

3. On a flat map, lines of _____ extend from side to side.

4. On a flat map, lines of _____ run from top to bottom.

On page 55, find the word that is not used. Rewrite the sentence in which it appears using the definition instead of the word.

CRITICAL THINKING

SEQUENCE OF EVENTS

Put B in front of the sentences below if they happened *before* Frémont resigned from the army. Put A if the events describe an event that happened *after* Frémont resigned from the army.

_____ 1. Frémont became the Republican Party's candidate for president.

_____ 2. Frémont planted the American flag on the what he thought was the highest peak in the Rockies.

_____ 3. Frémont recognized and named the Great Basin.

_____ 4. Frémont became one of California's first senators.

_____ 5. Frémont married Jessie Benton.

_____ 6. Two of Frémont's men went mad with fear during a winter mountain crossing.

_____ 7. Frémont added a t and an accented e to his last name.

WORKING WITH PRIMARY SOURCES

Read the description of Frémont below. Answer the questions that follow.

Obviously he is made of iron and accustomed to physical fatigue. His face, surrounded by graying hair and bears is thin, dark and tired, yet full of vivacity and intelligence."

1. How would a man "made of iron" appear?

___ a. chubby   _____ b. feeble   ____ c. strong

2. How would a man "accustomed to physical fatigue" appear?

___ a. soft   ____ b. determined   _____ c. silly

3. By reading the words around it, what do you think "vivacity" means?

____ a. dishonesty   _____ b. energy   ____ c. laziness

4. How do the writer's words seem to disagree with each other?

_____

WRITING

Compare the description of Fremont above with the sketch of a young Fremont on page 54. In your history journal, sketch your impression of Fremont's face at age 50.

CHAPTER 10

TEXAS: TEMPTING AND BEAUTIFUL

SUMMARY *First, the Spanish took what is now Texas from the Indians. Then anglos and tejanos (Mexican Texans) took it from Mexico. For nearly a decade, Texas existed as an independent republic.*

ACCESS

This chapter introduces historical events in the Texas War for Independence. In your history journal, make a cause and effect chart like the one on page 9. For the first cause, write Stephen Austin led settlers to Texas in 1821. List the effect. What was the cause that resulted from the first effect? Fill in at least five problems that resulted in Texas winning its independence from Mexico.

WITH A PARENT OR PARTNER Study the map on page 63. Compare it with maps on pages 23 and 41. What town appears on all three maps? What river appears on all three maps and is labeled on two?

WORD BANK   presidio   hacienda   vaquero   anglos

Complete the sentences below with words from Word Bank. One word is not used

1. A _____ is a fort in which soldiers live.

2. A _____ works on a ranch with "vacas," or cows.

3. A _____ is a very large house.

CRITICAL THINKING

MAKING INFERENCES

Put A if the sentence below described the battle of the Alamo. Put S if the sentence describes the battle of San Jacinto. Put B if the sentence described both battles

_____ 1. The Texans were outnumbered.

_____ 2. It was April of 1836.

_____ 3. It was March of 1836.

_____ 4. Santa Anna was in command of Mexican forces.

_____ 5. Sam Houston was in command of the Anglo troops.

_____ 6. One soldier, a few woman and children, and a slave survived.

_____ 7. They waited until the siesta hour to attack.

_____ 8. Travis, Crockett, Bowie, and the others held out for 12 days.

MAP

Study the map on page 63. Complete the sentences below.

1. About _____ of the northern border of Texas was formed by the _____ River

_____ a. 200 miles, Sabine _____ b. 600 miles, Red _____ c. 800 miles, Nueces

2. After the Mexican victory at the Alamo, Santa Anna led his troops _____ about _____ to Gonzales.

    ____ a. east, 150 miles   ____ b. north, 400 miles   ____ c. west, 200 miles.

3. The southern border of the disputed territory was formed by the _____

    ____ a. Nueces River.   ____ b. Sabine River.   ____ c. Rio Grande.

4. Texan troops marched _____ from _____ to _____ to defeat Santa Anna

    ____ a. west, San Antonio, Gonzales   ____ b. south, Santa Fe, San Antonio

    ____ c. east, Gonzales, San Jacinto

WRITING

Imagine that you could interview Davy Crockett before the battle of the Alamo begins. List five questions you would ask him. Then write the answers you think he might give. Remember: he liked to tell stories.

FIGHTING OVER A BORDER

SUMMARY *Hotheads on both sides of the Rio Grande itched to do battle. In the United States, the desire for land proved stronger than the desire for peace. The result was war.*

ACCESS

This chapter discusses the Mexican War that lasted from 1846 to 1848. To organize the information, copy the outline graphic organizer from page 8 into your history journal. For the main idea, write "War 1846–1848." For topics put "Causes," "American Support," "Battles," and "Outcome." Put at least two points under each topic.

WITH PARENT OR PARTNER Study the map on page 66. Compare it with the map on page 63. What river appears on both maps? What is the difference in each map's location of the "Disputed Territory"? Where would San Jacinto (from page 63) appear on page 66? Where is the Mississippi River on page 66?

WORD BANK   war hawk   aggression   treaty

Complete the sentences below with words from Word Bank. One word is not used

1. A person who supported attacking another country was known as a _____ in

    the 1800s.

2. Some wars are fought to protect a nation, but others are wars of _____ when

    one nation invades another.

In the dictionary look up the meaning of the word that is not used. Rewrite the sentence in which

    the word appears, using its definition.

CRITICAL THINKING

DRAWING CONCLUSIONS Each sentence below is taken from the words spoken or sung during the Mexican War. Put a check in front of all of the conclusions that can be drawn from each statement.

1. "Those who are in favor of the war . . . have succeeded in robbing Mexico of her territory."
    Frederick Douglass
    _____ a. Douglass disagreed with "those who are in favor of the war."
    _____ b. Douglass was glad the war "succeeded."
    _____ c. Douglass believed that Mexico had a right to the "territory" it lost.

2. "This is no war of defense, but one of unnecessary and offensive aggression." Henry Clay
    _____ a. Clay did not support the Mexican War.
    _____ b. Clay did not believe any war was justified.
    _____ c. Clay felt the U.S. was acting like a bully.

3. "When Zacharias Taylor gained the day . . . He made poor Santy run away." Song of American soldiers

_____ a. A leader who "gained the day" won a key battle.

_____ b. Soldiers did not respect their leaders.

_____ c. Santy was an American nickname for Santa Anna.

4. "Allow a president to invade a neighboring nation . . . and you allow him to make war at pleasure." Abraham Lincoln

_____ a. Lincoln believed a president should be allowed to make war.

_____ b. Lincoln was referring to Mexico with the words "neighboring nation."

_____ c. Lincoln was speaking against the war.

MAP

Study the map on page 66. Complete the sentences below.

1. U.S. forces traveled about _____ across the _____ from New Orleans to Mexico.

_____ a. 600 miles, Gulf of Mexico _____ b. 300 miles, Rio Grande _____ c. 800 miles, Pacific Ocean

2. U.S. forces traveled about _____ on the _____ from Los Angeles to Monterey.

_____ a. 600 miles, Gila River _____ b. 300 miles, Pacific Ocean _____ c. 200 miles, Gulf of Mexico

3. Most of the battles of the war were fought in _____ Mexico and _____ California.

_____ a. eastern, western _____ b. western, eastern _____ c. plains of, valleys of

4. Part of the southern border of the territory ceded by Mexico was formed by the _____

_____ a. Rio Grande. _____ b. Pacific Ocean. _____ c. Gila River.

WRITING

Study the painting "War News from Mexico" on page 65. Imagine that you could stand on that porch and read a news report. What would the headline say? What would the first paragraph of the news article tell you?

Headline _____

Opening paragraph (four sentences)

_____

_____

_____

CHAPTER 12
THERE'S GOLD IN THEM HILLS

SUMMARY *The ink had barely dried on the Treaty of Guadalupe Hidalgo when a single word blazed across the headlines: Gold! The word proved a magnet as people scrambled to California.*

ACCESS

This chapter describes the California Gold Rush of 1849. To help understand the importance of this key event the history of California and the United States, make a K-W-L graphic organizer in your history journal like the one on page 8. In the "What I Know" column write what you know about these gold rush. In the "What I Want to Know" column, write three questions you have about the gold rush. After you read the chapter, fill out the "What I Learned" column with answers to your questions and other information.

WHAT DO YOU KNOW? How far is San Francisco from your town or city? What direction is it? How far is Sacramento? The American River?

WORD BANK   prospector   forty-niner   nativism   Know-Nothings   lithograph

Complete the sentences below with words from Word Bank above. One word is not used.

1. A _____ was the nickname given to someone who traveled to California in

   after gold was discovered in 1849.

2. A miner was also called a _____ during the gold rush.

3. The _____, who called themselves the American party, based their politics

   on _____, a belief that only white Protestants were true Americans.

In a dictionary, look up the word that was not used. What other words have the same last syllable?

_____

Find the caption where the word is used. Rewrite the sentence in the chapter in which the word appears using the definition.

_____

CRITICAL THINKING

MAIN IDEA AND SUPPORTING DETAILS Each sentence in italics below states a main idea from the chapter. Put a check mark in the blank in front of the ONE sentence that DOES NOT support or tell more about the main idea.

1. *The cheapest way to go, and so the route most people took, was overland.*

   _____ a. That was difficult—you know that—but each year it got a little easier.

   _____ b. Once you were in California, your cares would be over.

   _____ c. At least, it was easier if you had enough sense to get to California before the snows

           made the Sierra Nevada just about impassable.

2. *In 1848, there were 812 people living in San Francisco.*

_____ a. There's an economic law called the law of supply and demand.

_____ b. Two years later, San Francisco was a city of 25,000.

_____ c. In 1848, 400 settlers arrived in California looking for land.

3. *At first, they panned for gold.*

_____ a. They washed gravel and sand from the streams.

_____ b. If there was gold, it sank to the bottom of the pan, because gold is heavier than sand.

_____ c. But it was stories of the lucky miners that filled the newspapers and that kept people coming.

4. *San Francisco had an assorted population.*

_____ a. Sometimes all those different people got along well.

_____ b. So things got mighty expensive.

_____ c. Sometimes things got rough.

PRIMARY SOURCES

Read the letter below. Answer the questions that follow.

> I start at 4 o'clock in the morning and keep on till 12 noon. . . . I rest for three or four hours . . . and then work again till 8 o'clock. . . . The nights are exceedingly cold . . We live in tents; I have not been inside a house since April 1. The ground is our bed.

1. About how many hours per day did the prospector work?

_____ a. eight   _____ b. eighteen   _____ a. twelve

2. What can you definitely assume from the statement above?

____ a. The prospector found gold every day.

____ b. The weather was always sunny.

____ c. The prospector worked in the dark.

3. What is a modern that means about the same as exceedingly?

_____ a. extremely   ____ b. deadly   ____ c. somewhat

4. From the passage above, what can you assume the prospector did not do very often?

_____ a. eat   ____ b. rest   ____ c. bathe

WRITING

Choose one of the photos or engravings in the chapter, and imagine you are in it. Write a "postcard message" or short note to friends and family back home explaining the circumstances.

_____

_____

_____

LIBRARY / MEDIA CENTER RESEARCH LOG

NAME _____   DUE DATE _____

What I Need to Find

I need to use:
- [ ] primary
- [ ] secondary

sources.

Places I Know to Look

Brainstorm: Other Sources and Places to Look

WHAT I FOUND

Title/Author/Location (call # or URL)

- [ ] Book/Periodical
- [ ] Website
- [ ] Other

- [ ] Primary Source
- [ ] Secondary Source

How I Found it

- [ ] Suggestion
- [ ] Library Catalog
- [ ] Browsing
- [ ] Internet Search
- [ ] Web link

Rate each source from 1 (low) to 4 (high) in the categories below

helpful   relevant

LIBRARY / MEDIA CENTER RESEARCH LOG

What I Need to Find

I need to use:
- ☐ primary
- ☐ secondary

☐ sources.

Places I **Know** to Look

Brainstorm: Other Sources and Places to Look

WHAT I FOUND

Title/Author/Location (call # or URL)

How I Found it

Suggestion	Library Catalog	Browsing	Internet Search	Web link

Primary Source · Secondary Source

Book/Periodical · Website · Other

Rate each source from 1 (low) to 4 (high) in the categories below

helpful · relevant

Printed in the USA
CPSIA information can be obtained
at www.ICGtesting.com
LVHW011321261023
762050LV00006B/9

9 780199 767335